It Started with Nails

by Karl Juergens
Illustrated by Tom Graham

PEARSON

Glenview, Illinois • Boston, Massachusetts • Chandler, Arizona
Upper Saddle River, New Jersey

Johannes wanted to be a carpenter. But he only had nails.

He needed tools. He needed wood. So he went to the market.

Johannes saw a man. "I have nails," said Johannes. "But I need wood."

"Fix my sign," said the man. "Then I will give you wood."

So Johannes did.

Next, Johannes saw a woman. "I need a hammer," said Johannes.

"Fix my roof," said the woman. "Then I will give you a hammer."

So Johannes did. He used a hammer. He used nails. He also used wood. He fixed the roof.

Next, Johannes saw a man. "I have nails, wood, and a hammer," Johannes said. "Now I need a saw."

saws

"Make a shelf for me," said the man. "Then I will give you a saw."
So Johannes did.

The next day, Johannes built his shop. He made a sign. The sign said: *Carpenter*.
Now he was a carpenter!